Twilight Hunt

A Seek-and-Find book

By Narelle Oliver

STAR BRIGHT BOOKS

NEW YORK

Acknowledgments

For their very generous assistance with my own crypsis research, I wish to thank:
  Debbie Scott Newman (Illinois Nature Preserves Commission)
  The staff at The Field Museum, Chicago, Illinois
  The staff and volunteers at Treehouse Wildlife Center, Brighton, Illinois

Published in the United States of America by Star Bright Books, Inc., New York.
The name Star Bright Books and the Star Bright Books logo are registered trademarks of Star Bright Books, Inc. Please visit www.starbrightbooks.com.

ISBN-13: 978-1-59572-107-5

Printed in China (WKT) 9 8 7 6 5 4 3 2 1

Library of Congress Cataloging-in-Publication Data

Oliver, Narelle, 1960-
  Twilight hunt / by Narelle Oliver.
    p. cm.
  ISBN-13: 978-1-59572-107-5
  ISBN-10: 1-59572-107-X
  1. Camouflage (Biology)--Juvenile literature. 2. Predatory animals--Juvenile literature. I. Title.

QL767.O55 2007
591.47'2--dc22

2006033812

For Mary and Phil Rowland, and Debbie and Barry Newman, in recognition of their care and preservation of wildlife habitat on either side of the planet. ~N.O.

"The study of camouflage is a slippery combination of science, experience, and blind fortuitous luck." ~Paul Zborowski

Harsh cries of hunger
pierce the cool air.

It is twilight.

The Screech Owl's
hunt must begin.

On silent wings, the Screech Owl flies...
watching for a flicker of movement,
listening for the faintest sound.

At that moment,
a Bark Moth flutters toward a tree.

Before the Screech Owl can snap it up,
 the moth has disappeared.

Nearby, a Katydid hops from leaf to leaf.

The Screech Owl follows, but in a flash,
the Katydid has vanished.

Like an arrow, a Praying Mantis
shoots down across the breeze.

In an instant, the Praying Mantis
is somewhere out of sight.

Meanwhile, a Geometer Moth
skims across the ground.

Only a second later, there is no sign of it.

Out from the leaves,
    a Green Treefrog long-jumps into view.

All of a sudden, the treefrog
is nowhere to be found.

Close by, an Eastern Fence Lizard
scuttles up a speckled rock.

In the twinkling of an eye,
there is no trace of it at all.

Up from the shadows, a Question Mark
Butterfly zig-zags to a branch above.

In the very next moment, the butterfly is gone.

Finally, a giant Luna Moth drifts
down through thorns and twigs.

There is no escape,
and it seems the hunt is over.

But overhead, a Great Horned Owl is watching.

Sensing danger, the Screech Owl swoops to land.

With feathers pulled tight and ear tufts high,
the Screech Owl has disappeared.

So the Great Horned Owl flies on.

The Screech Owl waits,
silent and still.

Then noiseless wingbeats
take the hunter home.

Can you find all the camouflaged creatures?

Page 8-9:

CAMOUFLAGED

  a) Cope's Gray Treefrog *(Hyla chrysoscelis)*
     Body length: 2 inches
  b) Great Bark Geometer *(Lytrosis unitaria)*
     Wingspan: 2 1/4 inches
     (appears uncamouflaged on page 7)
  c) Wavy-lined Emerald Moth *(Synchlora aerata)*
     Wingspan: 3/4 inch
  d) Inconspicuous Crab Spider *(Philodromus* spp.)
     Body length: 3/8 inch
  e) Brochymena *(Brochymena* spp.)
     Body length: 5/8 inch

NOT CAMOUFLAGED

  f) Angular-winged Katydid *(Microcentrum retinerve)*
     Body length: 2 inches

....

Page 10-11:

CAMOUFLAGED

  a) Dogface Butterfly *(Zerene cesonia)*
     Wingspan: 2 1/4 inches
  b) Buffalo Treehopper *(Stictocephala bisonia)*
     Body length: 3/8 inch
  c) Rough Green Snake *(Opheodrys aestivus)*
     Body length: 20 inches
  d) Green Stink Bug *(Acrosternum hilare)*
     Body length: 3/4 inch
  e) Angular-winged Katydid *(Microcentrum retinerve)*
     Body length: 2 inches
     (appears uncamouflaged on page 9)

NOT CAMOUFLAGED

  f) Praying Mantis (golden-tan form) *(Mantis religiosa)*
     Body length: 2 1/2 inches

....

Page 12-13:

CAMOUFLAGED

  a) Flower Spider *(Misumenops asperatus)*
     Body length: 1/4 inch
  b) Praying Mantis (golden-tan form) *(Mantis religiosa)*
     Body length: 2 1/2 inches
     (appears uncamouflaged on page 11)
  c) Black-and-yellow Argiope Spider *(Argiope aurantia)*
     Body length: 1 1/8 inches
  d) Giant Walkingstick *(Megaphasma dentricus)*
     Body length: 5 7/8 inches
  e) Goldenrod Spider *(Misumena vatia)*
     Body length: 3/8 inch
  f) Tulip Tree Beauty Moth *(Epimecis hortaria)*
     Wingspan: 2 inches
  g) Thrice-banded Crab Spider *(Xysticus triguttatus)*
     Body length: 1/4 inch

NOT CAMOUFLAGED

  h) Curve-toothed Geometer Moth *(Eutrapela clemataria)*
     Wingspan: 2 1/4 inches

Page 14-15:

CAMOUFLAGED
a) Northern Spring Peeper *(Hyla crucifer)*
Body length: 1 3/8 inches
b) White-footed Mouse *(Peromyscus leucopus)*
Body length: 3 1/2 inches
c) Curve-toothed Geometer Moth *(Eutrapela clemataria)*
Wingspan: 2 1/4 inches
(appears uncamouflaged on page 13)
d) Ground Skink *(Scincella lateralis)*
Total length: 5 1/8 inches
e) Forest Wolf Spider *(Lycosa gulosa)*
Body length: 1/2 inch
NOT CAMOUFLAGED
f) Green Treefrog *(Hyla cinerea)*
Body length: 2 inches

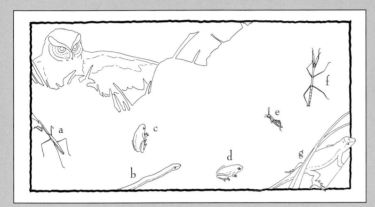

Page 16-17:

CAMOUFLAGED
a) Praying Mantis (green form) *(Mantis religiosa)*
Body length: 2 1/2 inches
b) Western Smooth Green Snake *(Opheodrys vernalis blanchardi)*
Body length: 18 inches
c) Green Treefrog *(Hyla cinerea)*
Body length: 2 inches
(appears uncamouflaged on page 15)
d) Blanchard's Cricket Frog *(Acris crepitans blanchardi)*
Total length: 1 1/2 inches
e) Obscure Birdwing Grasshopper *(Schistocerca obscura)*
Body length: 1 1/2 inches
f) Giant Walkingstick (green form) *(Megaphasma dentricus)*
Body length: 3 1/2 inches
NOT CAMOUFLAGED
g) Northern Fence Lizard *(Sceloporus undulatus hyacinthinus)*
Total length: 7 1/4 inches

Page 18-19:

CAMOUFLAGED
a) Northern Cricket Frog *(Acris crepitans)*
Body length: 1 1/2 inches
b) Inconspicuous Crab Spider *(Philodromus* spp.)
Body length: 3/8 inch
c) Northern Fence Lizard *(Sceloporus undulatus hyacinthinus)*
Total length: 7 1/4 inches
(appears uncamouflaged on page 17)
d) Brownish-gray Fishing Spider *(Dolomedes tenebrosus)*
Body length: 1 inch
e) Wavy-lined Emerald Moth *(Synchlora aerata)*
Wingspan: 3/4 inch
NOT CAMOUFLAGED
f) Question Mark Butterfly *(Polygonia interrogationis)*
Wingspan: 2 5/8 inches

Page 20-21:

CAMOUFLAGED
a) American Snout Butterfly *(Libytheana bachmanii)*
Wingspan: 1 7/8 inches
b) Northern Walkingstick *(Diapheromera femorata)*
Body length: 3 3/4 inches
c) Bola Spider *(Mastophora bisaccata)*
Total length: 1/2 inch
d) Question Mark Butterfly *(Polygonia interrogationis)*
Wingspan: 2 5/8 inches
(appears uncamouflaged on page 19)
e) Elongate Long-jawed Orb Weaver *(Tetragnatha elongata)*
Body length: 3/8 inch
f) Locust Treehopper *(Thelia bimaculata)*
Body length: 1/2 inch
NOT CAMOUFLAGED
g) Luna Moth *(Actias luna)*
Wingspan: 4 1/2 inches

31

CRYPSIS: THE TRICKERY OF CAMOUFLAGE AND DISGUISE

To survive on this planet, many animals must find ways to hide from their predators (those animals that will eat them), or to hide while they are stalking their own prey. One particularly fascinating way of hiding developed by a number of animals is that of crypsis. Crypsis works in two different ways: camouflage and disguise.

CAMOUFLAGE

Animals that use the camouflage technique blend in with their backgrounds through their color, patterning and tone. The Bark Moth (Great Bark Geometer), Northern Fence Lizard and Cope's Gray Treefrog are three creatures which use this technique. Often the animal's patterning breaks up its shape and outline. This can be through a random arrangement of colors or through a strong stripe or pattern which divides the animal's body shape into smaller, unrecognizable shapes. According to many studies, predators of insects memorize the shape of their favorite prey, and this becomes their "search image." However, if an insect's general shape is broken up by a strong pattern, it will not be associated with its predator's search image. (Zborowski, 1991, p.6)

To become really invisible, some of these animals use extra tricks; for example, some appear flat or two-dimensional on their backgrounds. This is achieved through "counter-shading." In normal circumstances, an uncamouflaged animal will appear three-dimensional (and therefore stick out from its background) because its lower sides will be in shadow (therefore appearing darker), while its upper middle section will be in sunlight (so appearing lighter). When a camouflaged animal is counter-shaded, its own coloring is darker on its upper middle section and lighter on its lower sides. This cancels out the effects of normal "shading" on the animal, and thus flattens its appearance. Many frogs are shaded in this way.

Even if an animal is well-camouflaged through its color, patterning, and the trick of counter-shading, it may still be visible because it is casting a shadow. To overcome this problem, some animals, such as certain butterflies, lean over so that their shadow is reduced. Other insects align themselves with the direction of the sunlight, and some creatures have a special flange-shaped edge which blends smoothly with the surface they are resting on, so no shadow is created. The Bark Moth (Great Bark Geometer) has such a flanged edge on its wings.

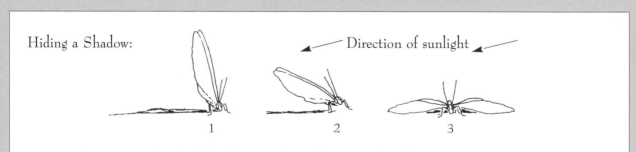

Hiding a Shadow: ◄———— Direction of sunlight ◄———

1. With wings upright, this butterfly casts a large, long, lateral shadow.
2. Leaning over, the shadow is reduced and mostly obscured by wings.
3. When the flanged edges of the wings merge with the surroundings, the shadow is completely hidden.

DISGUISE

Animals that use the disguise technique have developed features that help them to resemble an object (usually inedible) in their environment. In other words, they are "dressed up" to look like something else, such as a leaf or twig, which will not interest their predators. The Geometer Moth (Curve-toothed Geometer) and the Walkingstick use this disguise trick.

BEHAVIOR

Of course, none of these tricks of camouflage and disguise work unless the animals behave in a certain way. In most cases, they need to keep still, and they must use the correct posture. Some creatures use particular movements. The Rough Green Snake usually remains motionless among leaves and branches, relying on its coloration to avoid detection. However, if a slight wind moves the branches, the green snake will bend and wave like the surrounding foliage.

Although the distinction between camouflage and disguise is a useful one, there are many animals that rely on both techniques. The Angular-winged Katydid, for example, merges with a green leaf through its color and the pattern of veins on its wings, but its overall shape is also rather like a single leaf.

BIBLIOGRAPHY

Bomford, L. 1992. *Camouflage and Colour*. London: Boxtree.

Borror, D., and R. White. 1970. *A Field Guide to the Insects of America, North of Mexico (Peterson Field Guides)*. Boston: Houghton Mifflin Co.

Brackenbury, J. 1992. *Insects in Flight*. London: Blandford Press.

Denison, E., and B. Palmer. 1994. *Missouri's Oaks and Hickories*. Missouri: Conservation Commission of the State of Missouri.

Gehlbach, F.R. 1994. *The Eastern Screech Owl: Life History, Ecology, and Behavior in the Suburbs and Countryside*. College Station, TX: Texas A&M University Press.

Johnson, T.R. 1987. *The Amphibians and Reptiles of Missouri*. Jefferson City, Missouri: Missouri Dept of Conservation.

The National Audubon Society (Behler, J., and F.W. King,). 1981. *The National Audubon Society Field Guide to North American Reptiles and Amphibians*. New York: Knopf.

The National Audubon Society (Milne, L. and M. Milne). 1980. *The National Audubon Society Field Guide to North American Insects and Spiders*. New York: Knopf.

The National Audubon Society (Pyle, R.). 1981. *The National Audubon Society Field Guide to North American Butterflies*. New York: Knopf.

National Geographic Society. 1983. *National Geographic Society Field Guide to the Birds of North America, 4th Ed*. Washington D.C.: National Geographic Society.

Newman, D., R. Warner, and P. Mankin. 2003. *Creating Habitats and Homes for Illinois Wildlife*. Urbana, IL: Illinois Dept. of Natural Resources and University of Illinois Press.

Richard, J. and J. Heitzman. 1987. *Butterflies and Moths of Missouri*. Jefferson City, Missouri: Missouri Department of Conservation.

Zborowski, P. 1991. *Animals in Disguise: A Journey into Nature's Deceptions*. Sydney: Currawong Press.